The Vikings: 34 Fascinating Facts For Kids

Barry Magnusson

This book is just one of a series of "Fascinating Facts For Kids" books. For more fascinating facts about people, history, animals, and more please visit:

www.fascinatingfactsforkids.com

Contents

Who Were the Vikings?

1. The Vikings lived over 1,000 years ago in the northeastern European countries of Norway, Denmark, and Sweden, an area known as Scandinavia.

Scandinavia

2. For 300 years the Vikings terrorized the rest of Europe in their search for new lands, treasure, and slaves.

3. Although they were fierce warriors, the Vikings were also expert sailors, shipbuilders, craftsmen, and storytellers.

4. While many Viking families set up farms in the lands they conquered, others were great explorers and adventurers, and became the first Europeans to cross the Atlantic Ocean to reach North America.

Viking Ships

5.   The Vikings were master shipbuilders and constructed different types of ships for different uses. Cargo ships were wide and deep so that they could carry big loads. River boats and ferries were smaller and sturdy, with lots of room for passengers.

6.   The most famous type of Viking ship was the longship, which was built for war. Longships were long, slim, and very strong; and could sail through the sea at great speed.

A Viking longship

7. The longship had a sail and a mast to make use of the wind, but it could also be rowed by its crew using up to fifty oars.

8. The way that the longship was built meant that it was not just used on the sea. It could also sail quickly and quietly in the shallowest of waters, making it easy to attack coastal villages and taking them completely by surprise.

9. The Vikings were expert sailors and used the position of the stars at night, and the Sun during the day, to navigate across the sea. They also studied the movements of birds and fish, as well as the winds and sea currents to help work out exactly where they were.

Navigating by the stars

10. The longships were made from overlapping planks of oak which were joined together with iron nails. The mast was made from the trunk of a tall pine tree.

11. The Vikings carved fierce looking figureheads on many of their longships. Carvings of dragonheads were very popular, with snarling teeth and blazing eyes to scare their enemies.

12. A great deal is known about the longship, even though they can be over 1,000 years old. This is because many Viking ships were buried underground and the soil stopped the wood from rotting away.

Trade & Exploration

13. The Vikings traded with the people of many other countries. They bought wine and pottery from France, wheat and cloth from England, glass from Germany, jewelry from Russia, and spices from the Middle East.

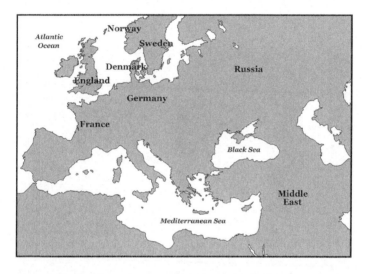

14. The Vikings often exchanged products such as animal furs, amber, and ivory for goods from other countries, although they also bought and sold using pieces of silver.

15. The Vikings also traded in slaves, capturing men and women on their raids and selling them in countries where slavery was practiced.

16. The Vikings were brave explorers, visiting countries all over Europe, Asia, and Africa. They also crossed the Atlantic Ocean, discovering Iceland, Greenland, and North America.

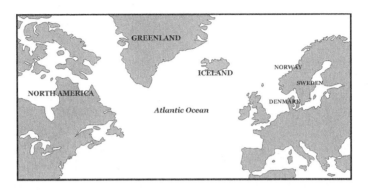

17. The Vikings often settled in the countries they visited, building new towns and villages to live in. They sometimes stole land from the local people, but they often lived peacefully with them.

18. The first settlers in Iceland farmed sheep in the fertile coastal areas. They exported the wool to other countries, along with other goods such as cloth, weapons, and cooking pots.

19. Greenland was first discovered by Erik the Red in 983 AD. It was cold and bleak with little farmland. Erik wanted other Vikings to settle with him in this new country, so he called it "Greenland" to encourage people to join him!

20. The more southerly countries of Europe provided a good climate and fertile farmland, although the Vikings settled everywhere from Iceland in the north to Sicily in the south.

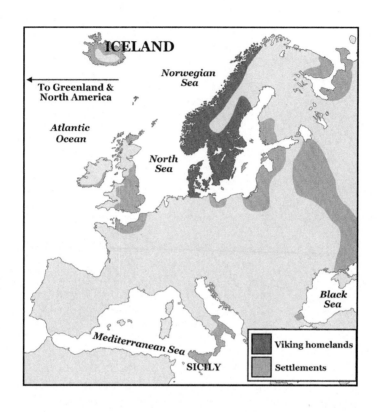

Daily Life at Home

21. Vikings were very good farmers and produced all the food they needed. They also hunted wild animals and caught fish to eat.

22. A Viking family would live in a long rectangular house made of wood which had a sloping roof made from grass. Inside there was a hearth in the middle of the house which provided light, warmth, and heat for cooking.

A modern reconstruction of a Viking house

23. The fire in the hearth was left burning all day which made the house very smoky, even though there was a hole in the roof to let the smoke out. There were no windows as they would have let in the cold, so Viking houses were also very dark inside.

24. In places like Iceland, where there were few trees to use for wood, the Vikings built their houses using stone foundations, with walls and roofs made from turf. Wooden panels on the walls inside would keep out the cold and damp.

25. Only rich Viking families had beds and chairs in their houses. Ordinary Vikings sat on benches or on the floor, and slept on rugs.

26. Vikings ate with wooden bowls, spoons, and knives. They ate meat, fish, vegetables, and fruit, and drank large amounts of beer. Wealthy Viking families also drank wines imported from Germany or France.

27. When they weren't farming or raiding other countries, the Vikings enjoyed their free time by fishing, swimming, and boating; and during the winter they went skiing, sledging, and skating.

28. The Vikings enjoyed story-telling. Their stories - called "sagas" - were passed down from generation to generation, and were about the gods, great battles, and great adventures. Some sagas were so long that they took days to be told.

29. There were no schools for Viking children to go to. Sons helped their fathers on the farm or in the workshop, and daughters helped their mothers with cooking, cleaning, and feeding the farm animals. They were also taught how to sew, spin, and weave.

Appearance

30. Vikings wore clothes made of wool to keep out the cold. A man wore a tunic and trousers, while a woman would wear a long dress covered by an over-dress. Both men and women wore boots made of leather.

31. Vikings wore cloaks which they lined with fur or goose feathers to help keep warm.

32. A Viking man held his cloak in place with a brooch pinned to his right shoulder. A woman wore two brooches, one on each shoulder, to attach the straps of her over-dress.

33. Jewelry was worn to display a Viking's wealth as well as to look good.

Viking Bracelets

34. Vikings liked to keep clean by bathing perhaps once a week! They bathed in clouds of steam which they created by pouring water onto hot stones. They loosened the dirt on their bodies by whipping themselves with twigs, and rinsed themselves by jumping into a pool of cold water.

Viking Warriors

35. The Vikings were fearless warriors who had weapons which were more deadly than anything used before.

36. Spears and axes were used, but the most popular weapon was the sword, a Viking's most treasured possession. Swords were often given names, such as "Leg Biter" or "Skull Splitter."

Viking Swords

37. Viking swords were strong and lethal, with a double-edged blade. The handle of the sword of a wealthy Viking was often decorated with gold or silver.

38. One group of Viking warriors was known as the "Berserks," who wore animal skins and charged furiously at the enemy, growling and howling like wolves.

39. Viking warriors started out by raiding towns and villages on the coasts of the North Sea and English Channel. One of the earliest raids took place in 793 AD, when a monastery was attacked on the island of Lindisfarne, just off the northeast coast of England. The raid was so brutal that it shocked the whole Christian world.

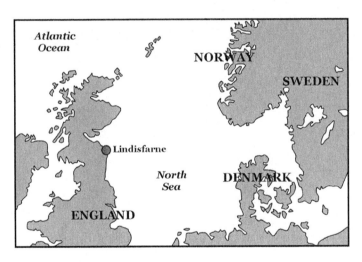

40. Soon the Vikings were sailing further inland on the great rivers of Europe, raiding towns and cities along the way. They often demanded large amounts of money to leave.

41. Eighty years after the attack on Lindisfarne, the Vikings had taken control of a large part of

England. Only the Kingdom of Wessex, ruled by Alfred the Great, held out against the raiders. Alfred eventually signed a treaty which gave much of the north and east of England to the Vikings. This new Viking land was called "Danelaw."

42. In 911 AD, a Viking chieftain named Rollo was given lands in northern France, and he and his warriors settled there. The area became known as "Normandy" - meaning "Land of the Northmen" - and many years later in 1066, a Norman army sailed across the English Channel under its leader, William, to conquer the whole of England.

William the Conqueror

Viking Religion

43. The Vikings worshipped many different gods and goddesses who lived in a place called Asgard. The only way to reach Asgard was over a rainbow bridge called Bifrost.

44. The ruler of the gods was called Odin, who was powerful and wise. He could transform himself into any animal or bird.

45. The favorite god of the Vikings was called Thor, who was the god of thunder. People thought that thunder and lightning happened when he rode his chariot across the sky.

Thor, the god of thunder

46. Thor carried a magical stone hammer which he used in battle. Thor called his hammer "Mjollnir," and many Vikings wore hammer-shaped jewelry to bring them good luck.

47. There was a mischievous god called Loki, and the Vikings would blame him when things went wrong.

48. The Vikings believed that if they died in battle they would be taken to a special place in Asgard called Valhalla. There, they would feast and drink every day in the afterlife.

49. Vikings who died of illness or old age went to a place called Niflheim, which was ruled over by a cruel goddess called Hel. This explains why Viking warriors were not afraid of being killed in battle.

Death & Burial

50. The early Vikings burned the bodies of their dead before burying the ashes. Later on, the unburned bodies of people began to be buried in the ground.

51. The Vikings believed that they would go to the next world when they died and so they were buried with things they might need there, such as clothes, food, weapons, and horses.

52. The wealthiest Vikings were buried in ships in which they would sail to the next world. The ships were loaded with their belongings, before being set on fire or buried under great mounds of earth.

53. The Vikings believed that the dead would come back to haunt them if they didn't treat them with respect, so dead bodies were washed and dressed before burial.

A Viking graveyard in Denmark

The End of the Vikings

54. In the late tenth century, the Vikings began to convert to Christianity and abandon the belief in the war-like gods. Viking raids died out and the warrior Vikings disappeared.

55. In the places where they had settled, many Vikings began to live among the local people, and their customs either merged with the local ones or disappeared completely.

56. In other places, Viking warrior chiefs started new and independent countries where they settled, and they lost touch with their Viking origins, creating their own new laws and lifestyles.

Assorted Viking Facts

57. Many Viking words are still used in the English language today, such as "egg," "gift," "sky," and "gap." Other words with Viking origins include "knife" (from the Norse "knifr"), "husband" ("husbandi"), "mistake" ("mistaka"), and "outlaw" ("utlag").

58. Some of our days of the week have Viking origins. Thor gave his name to Thursday (Thor's Day). Wednesday is named after Odin or "Woden" (Woden's Day). Tyr, a god of war gave his name to Tuesday (Tyr's Day), and the goddess of love, Freya gave Friday its name (Freya's Day).

59. Christmas has its origins with the Vikings, who exchanged gifts on the shortest day of the year. Their gods carried gifts in their chariots as they flew through the night sky, much Santa Claus or Father Christmas does on Christmas Eve these days.

60. Viking farmers shared their houses with their farm animals during the cold winter months so that people and animals could help keep each other warm.

61. Not many Vikings could read or write, but they had a form of alphabet made up of sixteen letters, which were called "runes." They had no paper or pens, and the runes had to be cut into stone or wood using a hammer and chisel.

62. There is a Viking cemetery in Denmark, near the city of Aalborg, which is one of the largest cemeteries in the world, containing nearly 700 graves.

The Viking cemetery near Aalborg

63. The Vikings were skilled metal-workers and the sharp, strong axes that they made were able to cut down huge amounts of trees which they used for building ships and houses. The land that was cleared of trees was then used for farming.

64. Although Vikings are often shown wearing horned helmets, the real Vikings wore pointed or round caps made from leather. Chieftains wore helmets made from iron, but there were no horns!

For more in the Fascinating Facts For Kids series, please visit:

www.fascinatingfactsforkids.com

Illustration Attributions

A Viking longship | Navigating by the stars (Fact 9)
User:Softeis [CC BY-SA 2.5
(https://creativecommons.org/licenses/by-sa/2.5)]
(changes made)

Longship figurehead (Fact 11)
nick hoke [CC BY 3.0
(https://creativecommons.org/licenses/by/3.0)] (changes
made)

A modern reconstruction of a Viking house
Sven Rosborn [CC BY 3.0
(https://creativecommons.org/licenses/by/3.0)]

Viking swords
Arild Nybø from Førde, Norway [CC BY-SA 2.0
(https://creativecommons.org/licenses/by-sa/2.0)]

William the Conqueror
John Pye [Public domain]
{{PD-US}}

Thor, the god of thunder
Mårten Eskil Winge [Public domain]
{{PD-US}}

Viking ship burning (Fact 52)
Anne Burgess [CC BY-SA 2.0
(https://creativecommons.org/licenses/by-sa/2.0)]

A Viking graveyard in Denmark
Gunnar Bach Pedersen [Public domain]

The Viking cemetery near Aalborg
Sjc
ShareAlike 3.0 Unported (CC BY-SA 3.0)
https://creativecommons.org/licenses/by-sa/3.0/deed.en

Printed in Great Britain
by Amazon